DON'T
BE A
D*CK

AN INTROVERT'S GUIDE ON THE
SUBTLE ART OF SALES

BRIAN J LAUDICK

ISBN 978-1-7349853-0-6 (print)
ISBN 978-1-7349853-1-3 (ebook)

"People don't buy what you do; they buy why you do it. And what you do simply proves what you believe."

-Simon Sinek

*"The most important thing in communication
is hearing what isn't said."*

-Peter Drucker

FOREWORD

September 21st, 2017: A day that forever changed the world of this introverted sales manager. I had contemplated quite a bit on how I wanted this day to go and how the training would unfold with my new account managers. Excitement was continuing to build up, knowing I was given free reign on how these rising stars were to be coached and mentored.

I was given the freedom to design a system/sales process for a new venture start up fitness center from the ground up. These two individuals were going to be molded however I saw fit and be the faces of this system and culture. What an exciting and scary experience to be a part of!

Where does one start when given such latitude? There were so many things to teach, so much knowledge to spill into them. I wanted to do it right, after all. This was an opportunity that isn't given to a lot of individuals, so I wanted to make the best of it.

Backtrack to the night before. I was sitting at the dinner table with my wife, Alyssia. I asked her where I should start and she said something that, at the time, I had no idea would greatly impact even the title of this very book you are reading now! She told me I should speak from the heart and look at why the teams I had worked with in the past were so successful.

It seemed pretty self-explanatory at the time, but the irony of it came to fruition as I was thinking of a name for the collection of thoughts that you read now. It was my epiphany.

I contemplated that evening on what factors truly played a role in the success of the teams I had been a part of. I was able to narrow it down to two major reasons that created the major underlying theme within this book. Before we dive into that, let's end this story first.

Fast-forward to the day of September 21st, 2017. I did exactly as my wife instructed. *I know, I'm a stellar husband for doing so.* We went through the first day of training, did some role-playing, some conversing back and forth... and when the day came down to an end, it was time to recap what we had collectively learned. I asked them both what their primary takeaway was from that day. Jokingly, Jen, one of the account managers, spoke up and told me, "Don't be a dick!"

We all got a good laugh at it and continued about our evenings afterwards, but she made a statement that really hit home for me on a more serious topic of sales. Which brings me to the two principles I had so passionately described to them earlier that day. Those same principles which made Jen use those four powerful words as her daily recap in a nutshell. "Don't be a dick." I continue to coach these two topics to this very day:

1. No matter the service or product, ensure someone becomes emotionally charged about what you're selling. Humans are emotional creatures. Emotion is very persuasive and is critical in the buying process. They have to see the value on how it will impact their lives and be able to envision that.

2. Build so much rapport and common ground with the potential buyers, entrenched in a genuine connection,

that they "feel like a dick" if they have to say no to you. (No, I am not recommending you make your prospect feel bad. That would be rude. Think of the internal dialogue of the prospect sitting in front of you. Do such an amazing job with them that they walk out of the door saying, "*Wow, I had an amazing experience just now. This will be something I have to consider and think about.*" Even if they don't purchase your product, they become a raving fan of yours.)

And so the idea for this book was born. All because my wife told me to speak from the heart and Jen made a joke about it. To this very day, it resonates with me during each tour I embark on. It sticks with me in every relationship I build, every life I positively impact, every person I meet. With my whole heart, I can admit that I will never be a dick!

So the question becomes: what does this have to do with you and how does this help you become more successful, make more money, close more deals, and change more lives for the better? It has everything to do with every single one of those items. As you read through the following chapters, you will be introduced to *the subtle art of sales.*

Whether you're someone new that's trying to get their "from home" Multi-Level-Marketing business going, someone that's been in the field wanting to continue to grow, or someone that thinks they already know everything and wants to read this just to see if you can find flaws in my opinions… I guarantee you'll take something away from this book that will not only push you to think outside the box on how sales really works, but will also help you get insight into how to approach aspects of life outside of sales.

Why listen to this particular introvert?

I'm 68% introverted according to multiple personality tests I've taken. I was deathly afraid of talking to anyone about a product when I was younger, and never in my life did I think I'd have the knowledge nor the confidence to write a book on a topic that most would believe would be written by extreme extroverts. If I can do it, so can you. So why listen to this guy from the midwest?

My sales career began well before I was selling anything. I'm a believer that everything in life happens for a specific reason and shapes us into who we need to become for the future. You may think that your sales career begins with your first sales job, your first deal you close, or even with this book. You'd be partially correct, but it doesn't tell your entire story.

For me, it started when I first got into lifting weights at the young age of sixteen years old. I was watching an infomercial on Cartoon Network during a random Saturday at one in the morning. The man flexing on the Bowflex was absolutely jacked out of his mind. I looked at myself and realized I definitely was not jacked. I had a lack of confidence stemming from my poor body image. I realized at that moment there would be a change I needed to make in my life.

I begged my father to buy a Bowflex so I could start working out. A few months into the uneducated/haphazard routine I made myself, I began to see results. To say I was excited was an extreme understatement. You can ask my buddy, Nick, who saw me flex my first forearm muscles in class one day.

Fast forward to eight years later after consistently working out. I had gained about 80lbs of muscle and started competing in bodybuilding shows. That skinny little kid with no confidence from eight years ago was now on stage in front of thousands of people, putting his body out there for everyone to judge. It was quite a change from what I was comfortable with doing when I was sixteen.

This is where my first life-changing event happened. One of my friends I had played video games with online for close to ten years shot me a note on social media. I had not spoken to him in probably three years at that point, so hearing from him was quite the surprise to me. I specifically remember his message to me being extremely long, but the part I remember most is the content within.

He began to explain how he'd been following along on my journey to become bigger, faster, stronger, and more confident. He let me know how excited he was for me and loved seeing the progress over the years. This all felt good and I enjoyed the appreciation, but here's where I fell into tears. I'm paraphrasing this, but below is what he told me:

Brian - I'm ashamed to admit I haven't been in a good spot in my life lately. It's been tough to stay positive when I feel so down on myself all the time. But, after seeing everything you've done on your journey… I decided to make a change in my own life. I recently started working out over the last 6 months and have already lost 30lbs. My clothes fit better, I have more energy, and I smile when I wake up and look at myself in the mirror. The reason I'm reaching out to you is, because all of the motivational posts you had, all of the workouts you showed, the changes you made… they inspired me to be more and be better. You changed my life.

Imagine reading something like that and not breaking down like a little boy. I replied back to him in tears and we started talking. He asked me why I had not made it a career to help other people in their goals like I had with my own. It was a really good question. A question that changed the course of my life.

When I received that note from him, I had recently graduated college and been working in the manufacturing industry for two years or so. The direction my life was going was a positive one. I was making great money for my age and had a fast track promotion to keep moving up. I had pretty much everything I could ask for at the time, but I felt compelled to find more.

That desire to want more kept eating at me from the inside out. Until one day, I thought it through and told everyone I was leaving my job there in Iowa to move to Kansas City and pursue a career in fitness. I had no job lined up, but when you feel something as strongly as I did then, you chase that dream.

So I left Iowa and moved into my uncle's basement in Kansas City until I could find a fitness career and get on my feet. I don't know about you, but the first thing I did when I moved to a new city was find a gym to workout at and find a grocery store to buy food from! Enter: 24 Hour Fitness - the first gym I joined down in Kansas City.

I worked as a bartender when I first moved to Kansas City since it was something I was comfortable with doing from when I was going to college. After two months of working out at a few of the 24 Hour Fitnesses, I built a few relationships inside the club. One of the gals at the front desk told me she thought I'd be a great fit and introduced me to the general manager at one of the locations. That two hour conversation with him was the next turning point in my transition towards sales.

He loved our chat so much that we nailed down an interview with the district manager that same week and I was hired on as a sales manager in-training for them! My first actual sales job and it was in a field I was extremely passionate about. That changed the projection of where my life would take me from there on out.

Fast forward one last time with me to the present: seven years after I landed that sales manager in-training role with 24 Hour Fitness. I've had the honor to work with some amazing and extremely smart individuals. Back to the original question of why even listen to a muscled-up small town guy over someone else?

Over the seven years of sales I've been blessed to experience, below are the highlights:

- Was responsible for managing direct relationships with a Fortune 500 company and helped steer the relationship with them by delivering a 5-star rating experience. That led to landing over $1,500,000 in closed business transactions to solidify part production in the plant.

- Led a team of 5 to be the top sales team in the district 8 months straight out of 12 clubs within 24 Hour Fitness. We crushed the budget every month.

- During those months, I sold over $100,000 in membership dues revenue and an average of $4,000 in personal training a month. I wasn't even required to sell training. Normally, it would take someone 2-3 years to sell that quantity within the company. Was recognized on the company's top performer's platform.

- Set up the entire sales structure and process for a brand new fitness center and developed a team that netted over 1,200 new members in the first year with almost zero formal paid marketing. All while maintaining a TRUE 5-star customer satisfaction rating.

- Sold over 100 memberships in the first month in sales at Life Time Fitness, netting over $20,000 in revenue within that month. Achieved top sales for the team in 1st two months and was immediately promoted to Sales Manager after 60 days on the job.

- Lastly, I have had the honor of training and mentoring teams of sales individuals over the last 5+ years that have continued on to be successful business owners of their own! That's where the passion lies.

Now that's enough about me. This book is meant for you and your story. Within these pages, we will dive into the world of sales from multiple perspectives, giving you the best opportunity to build relationships that last. Those relationships will allow you to fulfill dreams you never thought were possible. Now, let's get down to business. The learning begins here and now. Grab some coffee… It's time to close!

CHAPTER 1

LOVE WHAT YOU DO

ONE OF MY really close friends, Sam, was catching up with me recently when I was out on a business trip to Minneapolis for a week. He lived within two miles of the hotel I was staying at. Since I didn't have a vehicle, he was able to play the role of chauffeur. We went to get a bite to eat together and catch up on life since it had been a while since we last spoke in person. He's that friend of mine that always spurs intellectual conversation and gets my thinking gears grinding.

This specific evening, we were reflecting on the good old days, when we'd always have the chance to hang out. Eventually, we got on the topic of a job he had when he lived in Iowa. We were discussing what really triggered us to be great at what we do. He recalled being at that job in Iowa where he actually was pretty good at what he did, but he wasn't truly happy. His boss had a decently high emotional intelligence and picked up on that fact. Thus, he decided to pull him into the office one day.

It was a different type of conversation than you'd normally expect when your boss unexpectedly pulls you in for a "sit down and close the door" type conversation. He looked at him and was pointedly up-front with Sam and asked why he stuck around working there.

The question took my friend aback - not knowing how to reply to such a bold statement. His boss went on to explain that this wasn't a performance coaching conversation. He was doing his job just fine and there was nothing to discuss there. The problem was, he could tell that my friend wasn't fully invested and bought into the work he was doing. So he asked the question again. "*Why are you still here?*"

As he brought this up to me in conversation, it really was an eye opening moment for not only him, but a reminder to me as well. He realized that he wasn't truly passionate about what he did, and that showed. It didn't just show to his boss, but to his co-workers and his clients as well. Even though his performance wasn't necessarily being directly impacted by the lack of passion, he wasn't doing his job to his 100% capacity due to not being fully bought in.

I put this into perspective as I was looking at the sales world. I often joke with people and say I absolutely despise sales. They look at me like I'm crazy! How could someone that is writing a book and is so passionate about this VERY topic... despise sales? Maybe I was and am a little crazy - OR - maybe it's because I found that niche. I found a field that fueled such a large fire inside of me that a monsoon wouldn't be able to put it out. So much so that selling a service no longer felt like sales. It now felt like a duty and service to others that was going to positively impact the journey they were on, no matter where they were currently at. And THAT, my friends, is where major point #1 comes in.

You must have an absolute and undeniable passion for the product/service you sell in order to fully maximize your potential in selling that product/service.

Some may argue that if you are great at selling, you can sell anything. Which is completely true, to a point. But there's a threshold of success in any career. That threshold is what I like to call the 'point of transcendency'. *To transcend: To rise above or go beyond, to overpass or exceed.*

Let's focus on that point for one moment and use an example. We will pretend we have an all-around great salesperson that isn't overly passionate about his field, but is great at selling. He is in charge of getting (we will call this person "Bob") set up on a fitness membership and connecting him down his path to get to his goal of being able to lose 50lbs, gaining cardiovascular endurance to run around with his grandkids, and lower his blood pressure so he can go off of medication. We take that same scenario and have a second salesperson that is also great at selling, but actively participates in their own healthy way of living and has a story/background that they came from in their own fitness journey that instilled passion within them.

Both of these individuals get to know Bob, tour him, price pitch, and close him, but have drastically different results. Let's look at both from an artistic viewpoint and a scientific viewpoint: artistic, meaning people that tend to think with a "right brain" view on things and are more about creativity and human emotion/outcomes vs. scientific, which would be someone that dissects scenarios with a more analytical point of view.

ARTISTIC

Salesperson A: No passion   *Salesperson B: Passion*

Salesperson A: No passion	Salesperson B: Passion
Signs Bob up	Signs Bob up
Schedules initial orientation with trainer	Schedules initial orientation with trainer and gets him to purchase Personal Training package to jump-start
Does 1-2 follow ups potentially to see how things are going	Follows up regularly - relationship continues to build months after sale is complete
Asks for referrals - Bob says he will let salesperson know	Bob invites friends in and has salesperson B help change their life as well
Bob stays a member for nine months and loses some weight	Bob gets fully connected to numerous individuals specific towards his goals, stays for years, gets customized plan, goes off of BP meds, loses that 50lbs, and cries when his doctor says this is the healthiest he's ever been
	Salesperson B gets invited to events with Bob and relationship continues to build

SCIENTIFIC

Salesperson A Salesperson B

Makes $100 off of sale	Makes $130 off of sale since higher package was sold
	Makes $390 off of three referrals in first six months of Bob signing
	Gets Christmas/Bday gifts from Bob
	Gets positive review on social media for helping support Bob's journey
	Gets award and promotion from work for impact on members and gets bonus for them staying longer

Let's dig into this a little bit more now that we have a visual in place. Starting from the *art point of view*: when you look at it on paper, both salespeople achieve a positive result and get Bob signed up. They both are able to get him scheduled and set up with his first session with the trainers to help Bob get to his goals as well. Then, they both follow up to see how things are going to ensure Bob is getting to his goals. A job well done. We can go home and feel good about what we did for the day, right?

Until we dig deeper, we won't realize the impact of our initial impressions on Bob. In both scenarios, Bob gets set up with a membership and gets pushed along his way, but as we deep dive into both scenarios, we begin to see some distinct differences. You'll notice, in the scenario with the passionate salesperson, Bob gets started off with a package that gives him some additional personal training and tests to help him get jump started on his journey.

How that happens is where the distinct differences lie. Salesperson B has a story of their own within the product they are selling. They have lived the same journey that Bob is going through in their own way and know what it takes to get there. More importantly, they are bought-in on the product they are selling. When that happens, salesperson B becomes more open to the idea of diving deeper into Bob's history and getting to know him more. What makes Bob tick? Why is he here today? What happened to spur this exact time and day to come in? What has he done in the past? What does he enjoy? What has worked and what hasn't worked in the past?

There are plenty of questions we could go into, but the point (is) that salesperson B goes one or two steps further into the discovery. This results in them being able to discover the underlying story of how Bob got to where he is today as well as what he will need to be fulfilled moving forward. When you can find the true underlying core need of a consumer, you find the "golden nugget" that will help you bridge the gap between them being a naysayer and them being a raving fan of the product or service you provide. It doesn't end there, though.

Not only is the discovery process of the core need uncovered, but now the process of how value is built changes entirely. You can't customize an approach on "pitching" a product or service if you haven't done a great job building the backstory. Think of a really good movie you've watched in the past. One common theme you'll notice is that a great movie does an amazing job with building the backstory alongside the character development that led up to the timeline the movie is in. Once that is completed, the movie can effectively move into the primary arcing storyline and tie that into the climax and conclusion of the film. That wouldn't be possible without great backstory and discovery.

The next step would be the meat and potatoes of the film. Now both salespeople have the opportunity to take the discovery of Bob and write their own story as to how his experience will play out, how it's customized specifically for him, and what path he takes towards those goals after he signs up. In this scenario, salesperson A gets Bob signed up and set up with a trainer, but since the passion to drive discovery wasn't as effective, he doesn't have as much to customize for Bob on tour. When this happens, it's harder to create a grand vision on what will fully impact Bob in the most positive way for him and he doesn't connect the dots as well. Bob may have a base idea of what he needs to do, but the 'wow' factor doesn't impact Bob at all and the lack of motivation follows suit.

Salesperson B is effectively able to customize the tour and show Bob exactly what can be done and what the path to progress will look like in order to get to where he needs to be. This gives him hope and excitement that will catapult into his first session with the trainers and continue to grow as he sees that vision unfold. This also makes it easier for Bob to trust salesperson B since he's had his best interests at heart since the moment they met. That leads to a relationship that not only is great for the duration of their time together up front, but one that continues to build after the initial sale is completed.

This leads us to the last part of the movie, the climax and conclusion! This is where things really get exciting. At this point, salesperson A shows options to Bob and gets him excited enough to join up and start his journey. Not a bad job!

Salesperson B goes into detail specifically as to why having metabolic testing & one on one time with a professional for exercises specific to blood pressure reduction and weight reduction is beneficial. Bob starts his journey with a package deal that not only helps B make more money, but also helps Bob get more specific in his programming towards his goals.

The conclusion at the end is where salesperson B really shines. Both of them follow up on how workouts are going and how the goals are going, but salesperson B sees Bob in the club and stops to go through details of exactly what's going well and how life has treated him since. Bob sees dramatically different results from these scenarios and salesperson B gets additional referrals from Bob as a result of his experience. They continue a friendship that goes on to last a long time.

For those of you that are financially driven, we will briefly discuss the **science point of view** now. This is pretty easy when you break it down. Salesperson A makes commission on the sale and it ends there. They are onto the next prospect and sale. They net $100 for the close.

Salesperson B nets $130 for the close since they sell a higher package. Then they get three referrals in the next six months ($390). On top of that, the potential for promotion and the organic flow of clients coming in just from word of mouth creates revenue that can't even be quantified! Think about how compounded this effect becomes when salesperson B is doing this with every single person they are in front of. You don't have to have a doctorate in math to know the impact that can have.

Martin Luther King has a famous quote that I've always been fond of. It's his "street sweeper" speech:

"If a man is called to be a street sweeper, he should sweep streets even as Michaelangelo painted, or Beethoven composed music or Shakespeare wrote poetry. He should sweep streets so well that all

the hosts of heaven and earth will pause to say, 'Here lived a great street sweeper who did his job well.'" This quote embodies everything we discussed in this chapter. It brings our attention back to the primary focal point: If you're going to do something in life, you do it with 100% effort and with compassion. That drive, that energy… it's contagious. When you sell something you love, coupled with a passion for creating a phenomenal experience… Amazing things begin to happen.

Can you be great at sales and not have passion? Sure you can. Would you be able to fully maximize your return on investment and create ripple effects that help you and those you service? I'd say not.

Love what you do. Be bought in on what you sell. That's lesson one. If you don't currently have that, maybe this part of the book is a good stopping point. If you already have that fire lit and the passion is oozing out of you… Congratulations. Step one is complete. Now onto learning the subtle art of sales!

CHAPTER 2

IT'S NOT ABOUT YOU

I WANT YOU to think of acquaintances you've known in life and think about two specific individuals. Everyone has that best friend they would talk to about anything. Someone they can trust and confide in and be themselves with. It's an amazing feeling having someone like that in your life.

Everyone also knows that one person in their life that is the "one-upper". You know - That person who always has a story or response for everything you ever say. You could tell them that you were able to help a stranger walk across the street today and they would reply back by telling you they did the same thing last week and then proceeded to rescue a cat stranded in a tree 2 hours later, followed by feeding the homeless the very next day. Once they're done replying, you completely forgot what you told them in the first place to make them spew out everything they just told you. Oh, and you stopped listening two minutes ago.

Why do you view those two types of people so differently? Is it because person A is better looking, smells better, and likes the same movies as you? Probably not. You most likely are more attracted to the first person's personality more, because they are an active listener when engaged in conversation with you. They more than likely give support and are fully in the moment with you without detracting from what's going on in your world. *They take the time to listen.* This is a very important concept not only in interpersonal relationships in your private life, but is also extremely important in the sales world.

I can recall plenty of occasions in the past where a new salesperson definitely had the passion for their product or service, but was lacking on the second important factor in sales: *intentional active listening.*

A prime example would be a scenario I encountered a couple of years back. I was able to listen to a salesperson go through their process at a gym I was visiting. The potential buyer would say something about themselves, and instead of listening and digging deeper into the context of what the buyer was saying, the salesperson would 'feature dump' and have a reply ready.

"You like working out with people? I CAN'T WAIT TO SHOW YOU OUR CLASSES! They are amazing, you will love them." Then the potential buyer would say they enjoyed high intensity classes. The immediate response was, *"Oh yeah, we have a lot of high intensity classes. This is perfect for you."*

This back and forth style of conversation went on for the entirety of the sales process. The salesperson certainly had the energy to build motivation. They had the passion behind their words to convey faith in the product/service. They even showed the potential buyer everything they should participate in, but that prospect didn't purchase anything when it was all said and done.

What occurred in this scenario was a perfect example of point number two when it comes to sales. *It.Is.Not.About.You.*

Period. I know what you're thinking right now. *Brian, I never feature dump onto people or do back and forth banter like that. That's a pretty obvious thing to not do!* You would be surprised what you'll catch yourself doing, though. In this scenario, there were quite a few things going wrong, but let's break it down into just the big focus areas:

1. You don't have to reply to everything someone says with a feature of a product to build value. In fact, it usually takes away from the value and irritates the person with you, because they can tell how hard you're trying to "sell" the product.

2. They get the impression you're not truly listening to what they are saying. Which, let's be real, you really aren't. If you were, you would be asking more open ended questions.

3. People want to know about benefits, not features. That's great that you have a ton of classes. How does that BENEFIT me as the consumer? How do you know what I need to get out of classes? (Hint: You won't unless you ask.) In order to pitch BENEFITS, you have to get to know more about the person in front of you and their story.

4. People like talking about themselves. It's okay, you do too. No need to shy away from it. Great salespeople are good at allowing others to speak about themselves and guide the conversation in a way that's comfortable and relaxing for the person in front of them.

5. The less you talk at first, the better. That means they are speaking more frequently - and you, as the salesperson, are able to learn more about how you can *customize* the

conversation and experience to fulfill the need of the person sitting in front of you.

Let's pause for now. We have plenty of topics to look at during the scenario below. This time, we're going to make it about the person we are speaking with instead of about us. Since the Multi-Level Marketing world is blowing up right now, we can use an example of a healthy weight loss drink that we are pitching to a friend. We will have Bob be the example friend in this scenario and I will be the salesperson.

Brian: "Hey, Bob! How have you been lately? Have you been able to keep up with that little grandkid of yours since they were born?"

Bob: "Hey, Brian! I sure try. He has so much energy. It's hard to keep up sometimes!"

Brian: "I can imagine. They're so much fun to wrestle around with. I'm sure he loves grandpa chasing him down and wrestling around with him. Especially with the weather being so nice lately."

Bob: "Yeah all 2 minutes of it. I can't keep up lately."

Brian: "Really? What's been going on? Are you feeling okay?"

Bob: "Yeah, I'm feeling fine... It's just tough with all of my knee pain, you know? My lower back has been killing me too. I really need to lose some weight and get back into a routine again. Work has me missing workouts and eating fast food too often with having to travel all the time."

Brian: "I can only imagine how that must make you feel. How long have you been noticing the knee and back issues?"

Bob: "Since shortly after the travelling started for work. I just haven't had time to eat right, workout or anything."

Brian: "I'm sorry to hear that. It must be aggravating that you can't do what you want with him. What have you tried so far to help get you back on track again?"

Bob: "Not a lot, honestly. I try to pick healthy fast food options, but I'm always hungry if I eat salads or whatever I find."

Brian: "It sounds like you just need something that you can eat/drink on the go and fill you up as well, so you're not binge eating or having to feel hungry all the time."

Bob: "Yeah, I suppose so."

Brian: "You've been in shape before, Bob. It just takes baby steps getting back there. You know - I have a shake that I drink when I'm really busy at work and can't meal prep or warm anything up. It helps me stay full longer and would be great for you when you're traveling. You can just mix it with water and it'll fix the hunger issue while helping you maintain a healthy weight. Then, I can give you some meal ideas for "on the go" and get some workouts in with you when you're back in town. I'll give you a few samples to try out. Let me know what you think and I can show you how to get more once you try out the samples! Does that sound good?"

Bob: "Sounds great. I'm willing to try anything if it means I can run around with him and not be in pain."

Brian: "Of course! That's what is important is that he gets to spend as much quality time with you as possible and you're able to recover and feel better afterwards without too much recovery time. I'm excited for you. Let me know what you think!"

In this scenario, what did you see that was different? One huge difference is how the conversation flowed. There was no back and forth where Bob would say something he had an issue with and Brian would just pitch a product. It was a genuine conversation where Brian dug deeper into what was bothering Bob. If we don't know the root cause and we don't have that 'golden nugget' of what will drive Bob to want to try the product, our words fall on deaf ears.

Another thing was the lack of feature dumping. Notice how Brian didn't tell Bob about how it has 25g of protein per serving, is high in nutrients and is rich in fiber. He discussed exactly what benefits Bob would obtain if he took the product. Why? Because, that's what Bob cares about. He wants to know how it's going to help him.

It's comparable to car sales when trying to promote a specific vehicle. You don't just want to highlight all of the features and hope one sticks. You mention specific scenarios relevant to the person in front of you and refer back to what features will help them feel that and enjoy the experience you're referencing.

Lastly, Bob talked a lot. When Brian spoke, it was in reference to Bob's concerns and being empathetic towards his situation. Only once Brian fully felt he had a firm grasp of the scenario did he start going into the product. And he did it in a way that was genuine, in support of Bob's needs, and without coming off as 'pitchy'.

The dangers of preconceived notions

One of the largest mistakes people make in and out of the business world is stereotyping or creating preconceived notions. Everyone is guilty of this error. The reason it's so prominent in society is, because it's one of our core survivability mechanisms.

We take our prior experiences or what others we know have experienced in the past and store them in our memory banks in case we encounter it in the future.

This is great for things like remembering not to eat a berry that's poisonous in the wild. Maybe your cave-man friend ate some one time and he passed away the next morning. You instinctively remember that and whenever you see berries in the wild that look like the ones he ate, you're probably going to avoid them! This is why learning from mistakes and from history is so important.

The problem in today's society lies in the complexity of human interaction. We are in a civilized age. Unfortunately, we still have the same instincts and it can put us at a disadvantage as well. Let's use an example.

I'll use one that I encounter a lot in my field of business. I had recently started in the fitness industry as a Sales Manager and had a young lady come in to see the fitness center and tour with me. There were two things about this individual that I noticed immediately. She was wearing an employee t-shirt from a local fast food restaurant and she spoke very limited English. My Spanish was and is mediocre at best, so there were inherent concerns there.

I bring up those two specific items, because salespeople are all guilty of profiling individuals when they first speak or meet with them. It's a fact of life. It's near impossible not to do. When she walked in, I had a choice to make. I could assume that she had no money since she worked in fast food and wouldn't be able to understand the importance of what I was trying to convey verbally due to the language barrier, or I could start with a clean slate and approach the conversation as usual without preconceived notions. Boy am I glad I did the latter of the two, because it created an amazing story and a lifelong friend I still talk to.

This young lady spoke with me in "Spanglish" for forty-five minutes and ended up not only purchasing a membership, but thirty one-on-one personal training sessions as well to get her journey started. The importance of this? I could have easily given a subpar effort and done a disservice to her. She most likely would not have been given the proper instruction to succeed in her weight loss journey and may have never gained the confidence to be happy with who she was. Side note: she has lost over 70lbs and completely changed her life since we first met.

Another example stems from a huge pet-peeve of mine: when people don't put their carts back in the cart stall at retail and grocery stores. My preconceived notion is people that do so are lazy and not successful in life. I have judged a lot of people based on their ability to complete or not complete this simple function.

Recently, I was doing a live video with my wife on this exact topic. She brought up a point on that story. She said she sometimes will leave the cart by her car when she shops <u>alone</u>, because she's carrying our son in one arm, her purse in the other, and she isn't comfortable not having a way to protect herself if she's shopping alone and doesn't feel safe. So she leaves the cart there. I never really thought about it from that point of view before.

Another scenario to drive the point home. What if the person that left the cart in the lot had just received a phone call saying their family member was just rushed to the hospital and was in critical condition. Do you think the first thought on their mind was putting the cart in the stall? Probably not. They were concerned with the well-being of their family, which they should be!

This is where preconceived notions can get us into trouble. We assume we know a lot about a person in front of us based on OUR prior experiences with individuals or scenarios we've personally encountered in the past. The reality is that we honestly have no idea who that person is, what their history entails, where they come from, or what they are like on the inside.

In life and business, I urge caution when it comes to trying to make assumptions about the people you interact with. You never know what part of the story and journey of life they are currently on. Their experience with you could positively or negatively impact them in a far reaching manner. Every person you meet needs to be approached with a clean slate.

A lot of the items brought up here will be discussed in further detail as we move into the chapters, but here is a recap of what to take away here:

1. Listen more, talk less

2. Speak to gain understanding, not respond

3. Give benefits, not features

4. Appeal to their emotional connection

5. Don't have preconceived notions about people you interact with

6. It's NOT about you. It's about them. Don't make it about you. In case you didn't understand that already. Hopefully this drives that point home!

Now that the foundation of understanding is put into place for how you would begin conversations with an individual, we can start to dive a little deeper into what the ultimate goal of selling is to begin with. Let's see how that all plays into our process!

CHAPTER 3
SELL A SOLUTION/LOYALTY

WHEN SOMEONE ASKS you to name one or two brands that you have undying loyalty to, I can almost guarantee that you could rattle off a couple of brands that stick out in your head without even having to think about it. For me, it's Blizzard Entertainment or Texas Roadhouse. Food and games are close to my heart, so of course I'd be particular about what I play and where I eat.

Think of a brand that you love and enjoy. When you think about those one or two brands, what kind of qualities and characteristics come to mind? Maybe you enjoy the product/brand or maybe it does a good job at fulfilling a need. Texas Roadhouse, for example, is somewhere I know I can always go to have a good meal and enjoy the ambiance with friends and family when I want to.

There are many reasons why you may like a brand, but a vast majority of what makes those brands/products unique can be boiled down to two primary reasons: One: it provides a solution to a void or issue you may have. Two: that brand/

product is of high quality and is consistent in quality. You, as a consumer, don't have to wonder if the quality of service or product of the brand will be good the next time you turn to it for support or to use.

Blizzard entertainment has created great games since I was a young child. From the Diablo franchise, to World of Warcraft, to Starcraft, etc... Blizzard provided two things for me that solidified my loyalty for their products. The games they released were always of a higher quality, and they created an outlet of entertainment where I could get away and let my imagination run wild. In essence, they had consistent, high quality products that provided a solution to a need. Once the initial loyalty for the product was solidified, I would almost purchase a game from them before even knowing much about it, because I TRUSTED the fact that the end product would satisfy a need I needed fulfilled since it had always done so in the past as well.

The question is: *"How does all of this relate to my sales?"* And that is what we need to look at:

Selling a solution

The first of two parts for this section is regarding selling a solution. In order for someone to be fully bought into purchasing a product, they must have a need that requires a solution. Your goal is to ensure that the experience (you give) shows the prospect why your product or service best fits their needs. This seems like a simple concept, but the execution of the concept is much harder than what lies on the surface. Let's dive in, shall we?

Diving back into the fitness world for a real life example, let's compare two scenarios. Remember in Chapter 2, where we spoke about features vs. benefits? This is a similar mindset. When it comes to tours and the sales process in the fitness industry, you usually see two distinct types of tours. The first is what I like to call the *"museum tour"*. The second is an *"intentional tour"*.

The first type tends to take more of a feature approach to selling the product/service (in this case, a fitness center). What tends to happen here is the salesperson will get to know the individual's needs in front of them and may do a great job discovering a problem that needs solving, but when it comes to building value in how the product/service can solve the problem, it's very feature based. They will focus on explaining each portion of the club and make sure to point out areas that they feel would be of interest to the potential buyer based on the conversation they had during the "discovery" period. There's nothing wrong with this approach, per say, but there are so many missed opportunities when someone takes this route. It also is a very impersonal approach and causes the consumer to be less engaged, and therefore, less involved in the solution. This creates a gap where it is hard to build loyalty and trust with the person you are with.

The second approach is the "intentional tour". I call it this, because every portion of the process is intentional and has a connection point to building value in the product. This tour does the same thing up front when concerning discovery. The salesperson will get to know the individual, find the goal and the why (the problem that requires a solution) and get the necessary information to customize the experience moving forward. This is where things change.

When the tour commences, the focus is on the individual. It's less about pointing out each section of the club and making sure the product/service has what the potential buyer needs, and more about customizing how each section/area maximizes efficiency with use of time to get the potential buyer to their end result/goal (ie. solving their problem). One distinct difference is the salesperson will allow the potential buyer to engage more in the conversation. This allows the seller to get to know the needs of the prospect in more detail and allows them to build rapport/trust with the person in front of them throughout the process.

This type of tour will also utilize assumptive selling verbiage to ensure the potential buyer understands the impact of how taking advantage of certain parts of the club can impact their final goal in a positive manner. We will discuss this more later on.

What ends up happening with scenario two is a more personalized experience where not only is it easier to build rapport with the potential buyer, but the potential buyer also can fully *visualize* themselves accomplishing and fulfilling their problem with the solution the club and product can provide.

This scenario can be duplicated across any sales field you work in. The key takeaway is to realize you're selling a solution. In order to do so you must do a great job getting to know the prospect, their needs, the why behind those needs, and what aspects of your product/service are going to appeal most to them.

Loyalty

The second component to this chapter is loyalty. Building brand loyalty has two important components:

1. Up-front process/experience *prior* to the sale

2. Follow-Up process/experience *after* the sale

Pretty easy, right? If only it were that simple! The two parts of loyalty are not rocket science, but must be executed <u>consistently</u> in order to be fully effective.

The up-front process and experience is related to what we've been speaking to in the first couple of chapters of the book thus far. Is the buyer receiving a <u>customized experience</u> that gives them clear line-of-sight into how they can solve their problem with your product/service? If so, this part tends to flow really well and will be the easier portion of the two for salespeople.

It is a conglomerate of intentional questioning for understanding of a need, a customized solution specific to the individual you're working with, and a consistent execution of providing that customized solution.

The follow-up process is where the true work really begins and the true fruits of your labor really come from. This is often neglected by the mediocre salesperson, because it requires a time commitment that most don't understand the return on investment with. When you really look into it in depth, though, the time commitment isn't as much as you may think. And I guarantee you won't complain when you put it into practice and the dividends pay off for you.

I'm sure you may have heard endless amounts of quotes pertaining to the "snowball effect".

"A bad day leads to a bad week, which leads to a bad month, which leads to a bad year"

"One positive gesture can change the world"

"Start with the basics, then add one step at a time"

"It's the little things that count"

There are endless sayings and philosophies that speak to the *"snowball effect"*. When I reference that in the sales world, it's in regards to clients and potential clients. It really is the little things that count and add up.

Let's pretend we just made a sale at the gym. We have a

new member that just started their journey with you. Great job! Now that they have a membership, what do we do next? You'll usually have a 3-stage continuum in this part of the process. Where do you currently place yourself according to the continuum below?

Case Closed ⟶ *Fake it 'til you make It* ⟶ *Completionist*

Stage 1: Case Closed Mentality

In this stage, the salesperson wraps up the sale and immediately moves on to the next prospect. The mindset is surface-level based. *"If I can give a great up-front experience to everyone, the dominos will fall in line how they should."* This mindset can be perceived as a successful one, because numbers show for short periods of time and that person may also see positive reviews, but it's inconsistent and short lived.

This person will tend to still see success in business to some extent if they have a positive and outgoing personality that is likable. However, they may or may not ultimately get their client to their ultimate goal and TRULY satisfy the problem or need that person had. It is a short-term fix and can have a potentially negative impact on your business in the long term. This is true across all fields of sales.

Stage 2: Fake it until you make it

Stage two is a slight evolution of stage one. This person has the understanding that you shouldn't just sell someone something and then drop off the face of the planet like you never met them. They know they have to do some sort of follow up, and may do small things here or there, but don't have a true interest (or know how) to fully execute the follow-up process.

This person will execute minor tasks, such as send a thank you card to the buyer a week down the road. They might also do one reach out follow up to see how the product or service is doing in providing the solution to the need that the buyer had initially. It usually stops shortly after that, whether due to lack of knowledge of proper procedures or due to lack of perceived time. Maybe the salesperson lacks the care factor to want to progress further. They are feigning the connection with the individual and pretending just long enough to feel like they've done a good job. They will be more successful than the Stage 1 salespeople, but still haven't reached their potential.

Stage 3: Completionist

Stage 3 requires the most time and effort. If you take shortcuts, no need to read this part. (Pausing here for a minute).

Still here, huh? Let's continue on then!

Stage 3 is where the magic really happens. This individual takes what Stage 2 does and elevates it to the next level. Let's use an example in the fitness industry that we can custom tailor to all sales industries.

- Upon completion of the sale, the salesperson immediately sends a recap of their experience together and the showcases that active listening and customization occurred during their time together.

- A thank you is sent in some shape or form within the first 10 days of the sale.

- A follow-up cadence is scheduled to ensure the experience promised is fully being provided (this will vary on industry). I personally prefer a 10 day, 20 day, 30 day, and 60 day follow up on clients I sign up to ensure the experiences are positive and they have the resources and know-how to overcome roadblocks.

- Varied touch-bases occur to see how life is. This will also vary on industry. A great example here is my realtor and friend, Drew. Every year, he invites me and my wife to a Royals game and also gets us a pie for Thanksgiving. He never misses a year.

The evolution from each stage to the next ultimately comes down to a matter of will power. Which is why it is so important that you <u>love what you do.</u> It's mind-boggling how all of these varying factors work hand in hand, isn't it?! (*Rhetorical question alert*) If you love what you do, you will have a much larger vested interest in your clients and their satisfaction of your product/service. Make sure their needs and wants are as important, if not more important, than your own. The world has a crazy way of supporting you when you help others achieve their goals and fulfill their needs. Hopefully writing this book gives me some good karma!

Extra Credit

Selling a solution and creating brand loyalty are obviously extremely important. There is a specific Ted Talk that does a great job complimenting the core foundation of this chapter. I have drawn a lot of personal/professional development learning from Simon Sinek. If you don't know who he is right now as you read this book, you'll thank me later once you look him up. Youtube his video on "Start with the why". In this Ted Talk, he goes through starting everything you do with your "why". I won't spoil the video - you'll have to watch it yourself! This is what you need to take away that the video discusses:

People don't buy WHAT you sell, they buy WHY you sell it. The entire foundation of this book is taught through the understanding that you have a purpose and are FULLY bought in on what you're selling. There must be a true why and vision behind it. Only then will you truly see long-lasting success. Do I sound like a broken record yet? Great. Grab a gulp of coffee. This next chapter gets pretty serious.

CHAPTER 4

SWAT ANALOGY

ONE OF MY favorite ideals to mentor on (deals) with overcoming objections. For those of you reading this that have been in sales for some time already, you hopefully see the irony in that. *"Brian - Don't great salespeople spend less time overcoming objections than newer salespeople?"* You would be correct in thinking that, if it was indeed on your mind!

One of the most dreaded parts of sales (whether some like to admit it or not) is rejection. Evolutionary psychologists believe it started from the early days of hunting and gathering. Our brains are wired to tell us when we may become rejected by the tribe and left alone. Back in the day, this was a death sentence in the wild.

Another amazing fact: rejection activates the same parts of the brain as when we are in physical pain. This is why it hurts so much when someone says no to us as we are trying to sell something.

Once you've been in the business of sales long enough, and had the opportunity to coach and mentor enough individuals, you'll begin to notice a distinct pattern. Those that don't make it in sales usually don't see success due to two primary reasons: fear of rejection and/or poor work ethic.

I would need more fingers on my hands to count how many people I've seen attempt sales and never see success. It wasn't due to a lack of *wanting* to be successful in most cases. It was due to the fact that most people fear rejection more than they value selling something. This is why it is *so* important to have a foundational WHY and a LOVE for what you do. It'll help you build the thick skin and the resilience to weather the storm and build a resistance to the naysayers. This is a principle that helps you in life well beyond just in sales.

You're on the SWAT team - Time to infiltrate the objection 'house'

Have you ever watched a movie or a TV show where they have a SWAT team or military unit raid a high value target house? Of course you have! If not, watch *Zero Dark 30* now. Then come back so this correlation makes sense and my amazing art skills and diagrams coming up are more appreciated.

In any home raid, there normally are some pretty high level objectives in mind that need to be accomplished at all costs. It usually involves neutralizing a target of some sort, and mitigating risk to innocent bystanders, as well as your team. That objective comes backed by a solid game plan on how that raid should go, what will be done during the raid, and what should be done if complications arise… ALL with the goal of being as *effective & efficient* as possible.

Sales is no different than SWAT/military raids. At least in concept. There aren't explosions, guns, and door bashing in our example below, but the process behind the execution remains the same.

This is where the analogy comes in. Get yourself a black jumpsuit from Batman's collection and a nerf gun: We're going in hot!

SWAT TIME

If you're like me and are not lucky enough to have a full replica Batman suit, all is not lost. At least you have the knowledge to overcome objections at your fingertips. Let us begin!

When a SWAT team raids a building, a couple of primary events are going to happen. These events set up the stage for our graph below. One: we are looking for primary targets (potential objections during sale) that we have to eliminate. We do this through *intentional questions/discovery*. Two: we close the door where those objections lie to prevent them from coming back up later. If they do, we have a backup plan in place. Three: we ensure all targets (objections) are neutralized before yelling "CLEAR" to indicate we are good to proceed out of the house (to proceed to the point of sale).

Now that we have a base idea of how to read the graph, let's dive into it. I will be using an example based out of the fitness industry, but this graph can be customized and morphed for any product or service. Below, we will outline how it works:

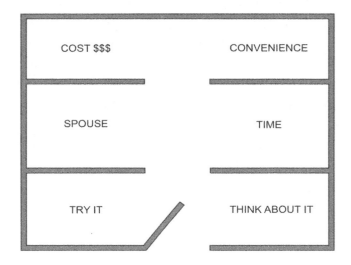

As you can see in the graph above, you will have a building with six rooms in it. Each room has a "target" or "objection" that we have to identify and neutralize before the end of our experience and getting to the sale. Think of your sales process like you would a SWAT raid. Each objection can potentially derail you and prevent the ultimate goal; which for us is solving a problem for the prospect. As sales professionals, we must be able to foresee potential concerns and mitigate them before they shoot us in the back! (Metaphorically speaking, of course.)

Continuing to use the fitness world as our example: You treat the sales process as if it were the home raid depicted above. A prospect walks in and you are the one that is going to give them the experience. Think of their mind and thoughts as the house and the rooms within the house. This prospect walks in with past experiences, preconceived notions, fears, goals, expectations, etc. You get the point. Prospects all come in with a NEED. It is your job to ensure that need is fulfilled and that you are the BEST catalyst to ensure that fulfillment.

You begin with getting to know more about the person in an organic way. I have found that being honest and forthcoming is the best approach with most individuals. Ensure the individual knows that this time is about them, not about you. That's when the discovery process begins.

Why today, why here? There is a story behind what brought them to this exact moment. For some, they may be open right away about it. For others, it may take some warming up to you and some getting to know you before they truly give you their "golden nugget".

The point of *discovery* in the initial meet and greet is two fold: Get to know them and their needs in a personable way, and be able to isolate and DESTROY potential objections that may show up down the road.

If you refer back to the graph made for fitness, you'll recall the six potential objections that normally come up during or at the end of tour. Each objection can be reconciled prior to them even bringing it up! Let's go through each one to gain a better understanding of how to approach using this exercise. Below, you will have statements or questions that can help alleviate the objection in bold text.

Convenience: Welcome into the club! Is this close to home or close to work for you?

Spouse: The membership is for you and your wife. Awesome! She isn't here with you today. Do you have a good idea of what she wants to accomplish with her health and what she'd like to have to support that goal? Does she have confidence in your judgement to make the proper decision on what's best?

Time: With the goals you have in mind, how much time do you think you'll need to devote to your health? (Does that match up with reality and what it actually will take?) Does their schedule allow for that?

Try it: Would you mind if I showed you how to use these TRX bands since you mentioned low impact exercise? You'll absolutely love the style of workout these provide while minimizing impact on your joints. What kind of culture/ambiance do you like to see within a club you're a member at? What does that look like to you?

Think about it: There is no way to prevent this one from coming up with certain questions. You have to build value in your product through the multitude of paths explained in this book and resources outside of this book. IF this does come up, the best question is often the easiest: "Of course - not a problem at all. What was it you were wanting to think about?" OR, my favorite, "Tell me more!" If the prospect is telling you they want to think about it, they either need to see more value for the cost, you haven't answered all of their questions, or they still have concerns you haven't addressed.

Cost $: How much do you think a facility like this normally costs based on what you've seen and experienced in the past? (*This type of 'temperature gauge' question allows you to figure out expectations of the individual based upon what product/services in the industry they've used in the past. You can change direction of conversation based upon how they answer this. The ultimate bummer at the end of a presentation is when you get hit with a cost objection, because you didn't ask the right questions to get their ideal range or didn't build enough value in the product.*)

As you can see, the point of the exercise is to ask intentional questions that allow you to prevent objections from coming up at the end of the process where asking for the sale occurs.

Great salespeople are adept at reading the internal dialogue of the person they are working with. This allows them to direct the conversation down a path that is not only beneficial for the salesperson, but also for gaining insight that can help give the prospect a better experience that is fully customized for their needs.

Once you've mastered this art, the objection portion of the sales process (the one that we all despise and have a fear of) becomes a much smaller portion of the time you spend with the prospect. This creates a better experience for both parties. I recommend you write down your own version of this graph at the end of this chapter and put in the most common objections in your field. Think about intentional questions you could ask during the experience that will help prevent those objections from coming up, or allow you to ensure you can overcome them later!

Sometimes, you may still get an objection despite everything you've done to prevent it. There will be a lot of variables that come into play which will help dictate how far you push, how in depth of questions you ask, etc. The primary thing to maintain throughout this despised portion of the process is having the best interest of the prospect at heart. If you approach the entire experience with that frame of mind, your opportunity to overcome the objection greatly increases. Whether you overcome it today or a week down the road, it'll help you maintain that high level experience that's necessary.

So, what does one do if an objection still comes up? This is where discovery and customization become extremely important. Imagine, for a moment, that you didn't do a lot of in-depth discovery into the *why* behind the concern the person is having. In our case, let's say we know they want to lose 50lbs at the fitness club, but we don't know the true reason why. Now, say we get an objection that they want to think about it. What do we do to overcome that?

Someone that didn't do a lot of discovery may ask one of the questions I stated above and say *"tell me more"*, but may not get a real reason why or may not approach it properly. Pretend the reason the prospect wants to think about it is, because they are apprehensive about starting a journey again after they've tried before and failed. If you didn't know why they failed in the past and what caused it, you wouldn't have any way to speak to it during the objection from a position of genuine understanding. You may try to use a promotional sale to get them to sign up today vs. having a real conversation. Here's an example of what you could say, if you did the proper discovery.

"Pam - I can't even begin to imagine what you're feeling right now as you make this decision for yourself. I can only imagine it has to be tough for you. What I do know is that you have an amazing goal of losing 50lbs, and I know that having a support group and friends working out with you was crucial for your success. You also mentioned that losing 50lbs would allow you to be able to run around with your little man as he gets into sports. I know how important that is to you. With the passes I'm going to provide to your friends and with the training support you're getting, as well as the support I'll provide, I have no doubt in my mind that you WILL lose those 50lbs. You'll be confident again and be able to run around with your little boy. So, what do you say? Are you willing to do this together, knowing that your roadblocks you encountered the last couple of times will no longer be an issue?"

See how much impact that has on Pam? Imagine trying to utilize a promotion to get her to start her journey today instead, because you didn't have anything to speak to on her core concerns. You can't create that type of dialogue and customize everything if you didn't do an amazing job discovering more about the person you're working with.

To make this easier, let's break down that example into pieces. You'll encounter dozens of acronyms that use similar language, but this is the one I was taught initially and stuck with:

LAORA

Listen: to what the prospect is saying. WITHOUT the intention of replying. Truly listen to the concern the individual has. You may have to dig a little to get the true concern here.

Agree: with what they are saying. The last thing you want to do is skip this step and try to overcome their issue. If they have an objection, it's for good reason. Empathize and relate to show you're in it with them.

Overcome: by building a customized experience, reiterating everything they wanted to solve by speaking with you. Show how you can eliminate their concerns.

Re-enthuse: and invoke emotion. Remember the two things I said you should be extremely good at in the introduction of the book? Get them passionate about fulfilling their specific needs.

Ask: Get their buy in. Ask again if they are willing to take the leap and move forward.

With this process, the key is to follow each step. The biggest mistake salespeople tend to run into is listening with the intention of replying and then completely skipping the 'agree' portion of the process and trying to overcome the objection right away. This is a recipe for disaster that causes the prospect's walls to come up, because they feel you don't have their true interests at heart.

If you follow the diagram in this chapter along with the LAORA acronym described above, I guarantee you will spend less time overcoming objections. This, in turn, lowers your introverted anxiety. That lowered anxiety makes you give better experiences to future prospects. Those better experiences lead to more referrals and <u>more time</u> for you to spend obtaining the *completionist* status and engaging in follow-up with active clients. It's the wondrous "snowball effect" in full motion! Maybe the small things do add up and matter? You tell me.

CHAPTER 5

IT'S OKAY TO GIVE FREE STUFF?

ALL ACROSS THE sales industry, there are metrics and standards employers monitor when looking at sales statistics. In the fitness world, we measure a wide variety of things. Those statistics are one of the major reasons I was promoted from a Sales Manager role and put into a General Manager role at 24 Hour Fitness in under nine months of employment. How's that's relative to this chapter, I'll explain in a moment! Patience, young sales-wan. (Yes, a *Star Wars* reference).

When I was employed by 24 Hour Fitness after first moving to Kansas City, I was hired on as a Sales Manager in training. To keep a drawn out story short, our team during that time frame was able to lead the district, out of twelve clubs, in total sales during eight out of nine months I was there. There was one month where we took second place by a mere couple of memberships. Congrats to the young man and his team that beat us that month. You know who you are! I'm still salty, by the way.

Within those nine months, numerous metrics were monitored. First visit closing, total overall conversion, initial personal training sessions scheduled, customer feedback rating, etc. When it all came down to it, though, it was about conversion and % to budget. And our team absolutely destroyed both indicators day in and day out. As an active Sales Manager, I was converting over 75% of my leads and selling an average of $4,000 in Personal Training a month on top of that, when it wasn't even required to do so in that role. I did so, because I was passionate about what I sold. I didn't even get compensated for it since I was an hourly employee!

Why is this all relevant? The company looked at me with a promotional opportunity due to numbers. Plain and simple. Sure, leadership goes into play, my team and how amazing they were comes into play, and the support from the other staff and their functions comes into play. At the end of the day, though, it's a numbers game.

All too often, we tend to be so FOCUSED on the numbers for this exact reason, that we forget about the overall experience of the person in front of us. Like a jealous ex desperate to get us back, sometimes focusing on the wrong thing (ie. the numbers) can lead us into hot water. We come off as desperate to the prospect, which is a huge turn off for them just like it is for the ex's.

Brian - how is this relevant to a chapter about free stuff?

Thank you for asking! The point is to give you a larger picture of how focusing on the full customized experience of the individual in front of you can impact your business. Too many salespeople are so focused on the sale and on getting that next lead that they aren't present in the moment and aren't *actively listening*. That can lead to someone saying no at the point of sale. And if you recall previous chapters… None of us enjoy rejection. It's painful!

If someone does say no to you or gives you an objection, how do you view it? Are you personally afraid to give them something for free if the objection isn't immediately able to be overcome at that exact moment? I used to be. A lot of us are at some point. I'm here to tell you - do not fall into that trap. Objections are not a 'no'. An objection simply tells you that you haven't built enough value to show that your product/service can solve a problem they want to fix, or they need elaboration on something you have not yet clarified.

I'm going to pick on MLM's (especially health-based product) companies for a moment. Don't chastise me, please! Being in the sales industry for the last seven years and having numerous jobs that have been people focused before that, I have met a lot of individuals. Many have approached me on opportunities with a product line they sell online and (to be frank) the approach a lot of them use has been distasteful or impersonal a lot of the time. And in most of those cases, they were quick to pitch their product as a gift from the Lord himself, but weren't able to provide samples of actual substance for me to trial and see for myself.

There is one exception I experienced recently. A gentleman called the main sales line at work and was inquiring about getting his personal supplement line on the shelves with our company. I was real with him in informing him that it may be tough to get that going and may be tough to get him in front of the right people, but I'd be happy to have him come in and experience the club and talk more on it. He decided to come in and was able to experience the club a few times and engage in a couple of conversations with me. After the second visit at the club, he stopped into my office to thank me for being so up front, polite and accommodating. He came in with a tub of protein and a bottle of natural testosterone boosters for me to try so I could give him feedback on the product. He also purchased a membership that day. This is important for a couple of reasons. One, this is a win/win for both parties. We were both willing to give something to the other for *free* in order to help support the other party; without hesitation. He enjoyed his experience and became a member, which helped me... and he gave me products to sample, because he knew I would like them and spread the word on them. In the end, we both gained something from giving out something free of charge.

The other key factor here is when someone is GIVEN something for free, they feel obligated to return the favor. I'm not saying to use this to your advantage... wait, yes I am. Use it. Subtlety ensure they see that you're going above and beyond to ensure they're taken care of. That goes a long way in making someone jump over the fence for you that may currently be on the fence.

When it comes to selling a product or service, the end result ultimately boils down to one major factor: trust. Do I, as the consumer, trust in you and your product/service to fulfill my needs? Are you able to showcase that in a manner that allows me to fully believe in and be happy with my purchase?

Sometimes, even if you do everything right, individuals may still not buy from you immediately. That doesn't mean you stop the process cold turkey and turn the other cheek. It means you find the root cause of what is preventing them from seeing the value and you pivot accordingly. Ensure the follow up process is what's best for the buyer and is set accordingly. Continue that customized experience. Sometimes, it means giving out something for free as a gesture of good faith to show that you're willing to back up what comes out of your mouth. Consumers just want to see that you are genuine and will follow through on your promises. Don't let pride or fear of rejection keep you from completing that.

Putting it all together for free

When you come to a point where the consumer gives you an objection, you need to ensure the following steps are followed and maintained:

- Narrow down the objection to one REAL primary reason. Make sure it isn't a smokescreen due to the fact that they don't want to be open about what's preventing them from saying yes. (Relate back to the LAORA acronym.)

- Provide a customized plan of attack for the consumer that will allow the objection to be remediated. This will change based upon the need of the consumer and the objection itself.

- Give clear and concise directions on how the consumer should utilize the free product/service so that it helps overcome the objection. Also communicate your plan to follow up to ensure they get the red-carpet treatment and an amazing experience (regardless of whether they buy or not).

- Ensure you thank them for their time (every time) and for allowing you to help serve them. After all, it's not about you.

It's one thing to give an amazing experience up front for someone when you're still trying to sell them something. It's another entire ball-game when you're giving an amazing experience, even if they don't buy. Those scenarios are where true trust is built. That is the differentiating factor that distinguishes the average Joe from the stand-out allstar. Which one do you want to be?

CHAPTER 6

THE PSYCHOLOGY OF SELLING

TRY TO RECALL a time when you encountered someone that did an amazing job at swaying you to see value in something. It could be a friend that gave a convincing argument on why they picked one player over another in fantasy football. Maybe it was your partner or significant other convincing you to see their point of view in an argument (assuming you were opening with the intention of understanding, not responding!) Maybe it was a salesperson that did an extremely good job at convincing you why that new peloton bike was going to be worth the investment and give you the dad bod you always dreamed of! (I kid. I've heard nothing but great things about them!) Think of a scenario like that.

Now, I want you to reflect back on that experience in your life and what key factors played a role in you being convinced to see their point of view. You may be able to recall something they said or how they said it that made you turn the corner, but not be able to explain how or why it actually happened. Don't you worry, young sales-wan. The psychological force within you will soon learn. Read and learn, you must!

Humans are selfish

The irony with selling is that it goes against human nature to be great at the art of sales. That's why 90% of people in the field usually end up leaving it and not seeing the success they want. It's hard. It's hard, because humans by nature are selfish creatures. Our core instincts are all based around self-preservation and survival. In a more modern day and age, you can correlate that with inflation of ego and making lots of money.

Imagine if all salespeople only took these core instincts into consideration and sold with their own interests in mind. What a world that would be. Nothing would ever sell and an economic crisis would unfold before us! No one would be engaging in active listening, have a genuine care for fulfilling a need of the person in front of them, and they certainly wouldn't be able to see how everything discussed in this book could impact their future self. They'd only be focused on the moment and in the present. They'd be focused on putting food on their family's table and a roof over their heads. This type of mentality can hamstring any hope of referral business or positive reviews on Yelp, I can assure you that!

Sales goes against everything your gut instincts naturally tell you to do. You must engage in thought patterns and behaviors that don't come naturally to a lot of individuals. This is not only important in the world of sales, but daily life as well. Better get your notepad out (or tablet for those operating in the 21st century). This chapter is going to give you some insight into your life and how you approach every interaction you have moving forward.

The Outline of Inception

If you're a movie buff like me, you appreciate a good movie reference. Sales reminds me a lot of the movie *Inception*. If you haven't seen this movie before, this would be a great stopping point again so you can understand the reference. I promise I want you to finish the book despite all these breaks I make you take.

In the movie, they plant a dream within a dream, within a dream. The premise is showing it is possible to implant a thought or an idea into someone's mind. If the 'mind-surfer' goes deep enough into the dreams, the idea organically feels like it came from the individual in which it was planted. (Stay with me here). I won't give away the movie, but instead direct your attention to how this is directly related to the psychology of sales.

You have to be able to convince your prospect that what you're selling is not only going to solve a problem they so desperately want to fix, but is also the BEST route in doing so. The kicker is accomplishing that process without the prospect realizing you're purposefully leading them down that path. It must feel like the prospect is convincing themselves on your product. And that, my friend, is where the <u>art</u> portion of sales comes into play. I could legitimately write an ENTIRE book on this subject and may very well do so eventually. For now, it'll suffice to go through the list of subjects below:

- A dream within a dream within a dream
- A little less talk and a lot more action
- It's all about telling a story
- Assumptive sales verbiage
- The fear of missing out

- Preventing loss
- Guiding the path (you are the light)

Let's break each of these down briefly. Once you've gone through this chapter, you will be so close to being a Jedi-Sales-Master that you can practically see things move as your mind wills it. It'll be like Mel Gibson in *What Women Want*. You'll feel like Neo in *The Matrix* when he finally realized his potential and stopped all of the incoming bullets in their tracks as they locked in on him. You'll... I think you get the point.

Principle 1: A dream within a dream within a dream

Recall when we spoke about the principle behind this statement. It is the catch-all for sales psychology. The entire process of selling is an art form and is NOT to be rushed. It cannot be hurried along. When the prospect gets to the final portion of the process and decides whether they want to purchase or not, the decision has to feel like it's coming from them. Deep down, you may have implanted thoughts and ideas in their head subtlety, but they must not feel your intrusion upon doing so. This is why it is so important that you sell with the intention of having their best interests at heart and sell something you love. The process becomes much more organic and the inception of the sale is much easier to accomplish. Now the question becomes: h*ow is that done exactly?* Continue reading to see!

Principle 2: A little less talk, and a lot more action!

Yes, this is meant to be a reference to the country song by Toby Keith. And yes, that probably dates me much like most of these references do.

The meaning behind this one is pretty straight forward. STOP TALKING SO MUCH WHEN YOU'RE TRYING TO SELL. Whoa, sorry. I got carried away for a moment. Let's rewind and pull material from earlier in the book. When you're engaged with a prospect, who is the focal point of the conversation? You'd be correct if you just said *the prospect is.* Great job! A little Psychology 101 for you: Recall a time where you were intrigued in a conversation and felt really good about how the discussion was going. One where you were able to give your input and have others listen to you. How did that feel?

It felt amazing. I don't even have to ask you how it felt. A vast majority of human beings LOVE to talk about themselves. It releases dopamine. That's why it feels like eating your favorite food or (yes, sex… almost) when you talk and are engaged in the conversation. The hormone release occurs almost immediately and takes hold. The point here is this: way too many salespeople talk about themselves or their product to the point where the prospect becomes uninterested and ultimately zones out mid conversation. Don't be that person. Get them engaged in dialogue. Let them tell you about themselves, about what they like to do, and about what their family is going to do this weekend. (Most likely watching Netflix since I'm currently writing this book while we're on Covid-19 lockdown.)

Principle 3: It's about telling a story...

Do me a favor right now and take a highlighter to this book or your tablet and highlight this one. If you want to really master the art of selling, this is one that is almost a lost art. Rarely do I meet people that engage in dialogue deeply entrenched enough with meaning to get me excited on a core level. Yet, it's one of the most important pieces in sales psychology.

Every person you meet, every interaction you have - It is guided by prior circumstances, events, experiences, etc.

Prospects you meet have been shaped and molded into their current state in this exact moment through a tedious complicated process called *life*. It's important to remember this fact when speaking to someone for the first time and engaging in conversation.

Even more important to YOU is how those life experiences shape the way they interact with you and how they will respond to your input. It's imperative value and trust is built with a prospect. For some prospects, that may take longer than others. Some will immediately open up to you, while others will initially be guarded and won't let their walls down until they know you have their best interests at heart.

The other portion of telling a story is exactly what the words entail. In the fitness world, this is related to their goals and why they stepped foot in that door to meet with me today. My goal is to uncover the true core reason for them being there. Where do they want their lives to be three months from now? A year from now? How does that look to them? Am I able to help them find that vision if they don't already have it and give them a clear line of sight to show them the way?

The other part of telling a story is being able to tell your story and become vulnerable yourself. People want to work with other people that are human and have a story of their own. Someone that has flaws and concerns of their own. By bringing down your own walls and becoming vulnerable, you give the prospect permission to do the same. They will be more comfortable sharing with you if you give them something personal about yourself in return.

Stories do amazing things in invoking emotion and passion. Remember when I said you should be REALLY amazing at two things, if nothing else? This is one of them. If you can invoke emotion and get someone to fully envision themselves overcoming the issue they have in the present day, you can sell anything to them.

Principle 4: Assumptive Sales Verbiage

This principle is a very simplistic one. It just takes practice to master. Let's start by using an example to clarify how the words you use can make such an impactful difference in the flow of conversation:

Scenario 1: "If you enjoy the support a group brings to you, I recommend our fitness class programs. I think you'll enjoy them and hopefully you find some that fit within your schedule. Do you think you maybe would want to try some out?! I really enjoy them when I take them!"

Scenario 2: "From what I'm hearing, having support is very important to you. I know you said you tried classes in the past and enjoyed them. I'm excited for you to take our upper body and lower body classes when you start with us! With your focal point being losing weight and toning your entire body, these two classes will give you a 1-2 punch that will launch you towards your goal of losing those 20lbs. More importantly, they will provide you with all the support you're looking for in your workouts with our amazing instructors and others in class pushing you. I'll help show you how to sign up for those once we get done today!"

What differences do you see in these two scenarios? In both, they reference what the prospect needs to have support in their workouts and show excitement towards the programming. They look pretty similar... right?

The large difference here lies within the word selection. In scenario one, you'll notice words such as: 'I think', 'if', 'maybe', 'hopefully'. In scenario two, it's 'I'm excited', 'when you', 'will', 'once we'. The context of the ones in scenario one are coming from a questioning standpoint. They are unsure. The context of scenario two words are definitive, confident and show vision.

The other large factor between the two scenarios is the ability to build a vision of the story that will play out once the prospect does sign up and buy the product. When done properly, the prospects are subconsciously already envisioning themselves using the product that is being sold. These small changes in wording and the context in which they are presented is a game changer!

Principle 5: Fear of Missing Out

Let's be real: Salespeople always hate seeing advertisements or promotions that say, "For a limited time only!" I personally can't stand it. Yet we still see these types of advertisements ALL OVER the place. Why is it that sales skyrocket during Black Friday? Why do we fall into the trap and buy things we may not otherwise have purchased during what should be just another day?

It works, because the tactic of scarcity is used. People genuinely have a fear of missing out. Missing out on that deal.

Missing out on the opportunity of having something that may only run limited production. It's why more people tend to be impressed when they see a Lamborghini drive by than when they see a Toyota Corolla pass by. (No offense to you if you own a Corolla.)

Use special events and have timelines on promotions, if you're able to have the leverage to do so with your product or services. Many top-end companies use limited production and time-based promotions to push products out the door. If it's always on special, then it's not really special. The same goes with the opposite. If you never act like you're running a promotion and increase urgency, then the prospect never has urgency to purchase.

Principle 6: Preventing Loss

You'll notice some extremely familiar similarities between principles five and six. Both operate with the same psychological profile. There's two ways to build value in making someone want to purchase something. The first is the one that most of us think about. That is the value of what the product/service can do for the prospect or potential buyer.

The second way to make someone want to purchase a product or service is by highlighting what opportunity they may miss or what they may regret if they DON'T purchase the product. It's pretty simple in the fitness world. What would the prospect in front of you feel if they didn't lose those 40lbs they wanted to? If they weren't able to have more confidence in themselves and run around with their children? That's a powerful thought.

Not only is it important that you highlight what the product/service can do to help someone; it's also important that you highlight what they could be missing out on if they choose not to purchase.

Principle 7: Guiding the Path (YOU are the light)

This last principle relates back to the very first principle of having a dream within a dream. You have to personally guide the prospect in conversation that allows them to truly see the value of how your product/service is the BEST one for them. You also have to do it without them realizing you're doing so. The idea has to be entrenched deep enough in conversation that they don't feel you guiding them down certain conversational paths.

This is accomplished by being genuine and engaging in real dialogue. You can't be robotic. Let's talk through the overcoming objections graph as reference for an example. In Chapter 4, we learned how to ask questions that are intentional and help us overcome potential objections. This can be done one of two ways. It can be robotic and impersonal (which often is how it comes across in inexperienced salespeople that have been taught from a script). Once you become more experienced through repetition, you can let the conversation flow naturally. This will ensure the path the discussion takes is allowing you to ask those intentional questions without seeming choppy or sounding like you're pre-structuring questions.

The other part of guiding the path is minimizing options at the point of sale. If your sales pitch is too convoluted and has too many options, it can create uncertainty in choosing the right option for them. I personally try to narrow down membership to two primary options, with me guiding them to the route I believe will better fit their needs and solve their problem. Use this when applicable.

Quite a few of these principles were actually used in *Inception* when the team was trying to plant their idea within multiple dreams. Psychological warfare was used to ensure the idea was his own, which made everything organic and work out in the end. Just make sure that you personally don't get lost in the dream with them and everything will work out just fine!

CHAPTER 7

The Chameleon
(Personality Profiling)

I ALWAYS FEEL like I'm a top secret FBI agent when going through the sales process. Trying to read people, their thought patterns and their personalities is exciting. I remember the second time I took the Meyers Briggs 16 personalities test to see what personality type I was. I was actually in my boss' office after completing it. It was being completed as a leadership exercise to allow everyone to get to know each other on a deeper level. I already knew what type I came up with last time, but was interested to see how it had changed over the last couple of years since I took it last. A lot of the core traits were very similar and when I showed the results to my boss, he started laughing.

He couldn't believe I was introverted. Someone in sales who loves to build relationships with others and is very outgoing, but 68% introverted? There must have been a flaw on the test.

Yet, here we were. And the results were perfectly accurate!

If you haven't taken that test before, I highly suggest you do. There's some great information to take away, and it gives some great insight into the next portion of our wonderful adventure: Understanding personality types and learning to adapt each type.

Experts will reference a multitude of names and titles for what we call the "4 core personalities", but the ideal behind each remains the same. For our purposes, I will just refer to them as listed below.

1. Dominant

2. Analytic

3. Influencer

4. Intuitive

As I'm sure you can imagine, it is extremely hard to narrow everyone's personality types into just 4 quadrants, but it makes it easier to coach individuals for understanding purposes. Let's take a look at each one in detail.

Type 1: Dominant

This type of individual is your stereotypical Type-A personality. They will seem pressed for time and want to see results from the conversation in a timely manner. They don't have time for small talk and will want to cut right to the chase. (I'm guilty of this, as this is my primary personality type when it comes to buying something). They are the ones that already did their research on your product well before reaching out to you and know exactly what they want.

How to deal with:

Be direct and to the point while maintaining professionalism. Be respectful of their time. Let them know you're there to help them make the process as painless and straightforward as possible. Radical candor and being real will go a long way with this type of person. Just give them what they want!

Type 2: Analytic

Analytical personalities are usually the most frustrating type to work with for most salespeople, because they tend to be extremely methodical in their thought processes and generally take longer to make a decision on buying. These are the ones that are going to tell you they need to 'think about it' and are the individuals who will require an extremely detailed and customized process in place to ensure any objection they have is reconciled in detailed fashion. They want to meticulously comb through every detail of the product and service to ensure it's absolutely the best thing for them. This can be a slow process.

How to deal with:

Analytic buyers just want to know that what you say has credibility and that they can trust you. The more consistent you are with communication and the more reliable you are in your follow through with what you say you will do, the better. If you follow through, stay patient, and provide them an amazing experience, they will eventually buy.

Type 3: Influencer

This type of individual enjoys life for the change and experiences it provides. They love to have a good time, trying new things, and are independent and strong-willed. Much like dominant personality types. The key difference with influencers is they enjoy stimulating conversation if it's fun and outside the box. They also value their freedom to make decisions on their own will. They would be one of the harder ones to plant an idea into with the inception concept.

How to deal with:

Have fun with them. Make the process entertaining while allowing them to talk more while you guide the direction subtlety. Help them understand you're here to give them a great experience and show them how your product/service will provide a fresh perspective to fulfilling their need; all while ultimately giving them the power to make the choice in that decision.

Type 4: Intuitive

These are my personal favorites to work with, because they enjoy the genuine connection aspect of the process and are people-oriented. They generally don't want someone pushy or confrontational and want to know how your product/service will help people change things for the better. They want you to take part in the journey and include you with them on theirs. If you have any hint of being robotic or scripted, do yourself a favor and turn that off. This prospect will want a genuine connection where you do a great job listening and supporting their needs.

How to deal with:

I already hit on this a lot within the description, but just to reiterate… Build a foundational friendship with them, turn off sales-mode, be a great listener, and take part in their journey to create a genuine connection with them. These are the people that will continue to reach out and talk to you well after the sale is completed and will be a walking billboard for your personal brand, if you give them a phenomenal experience.

Now that we have the four personality types out there and how to deal with them, we can look at this from a thousand foot view. Let's go back to the beginning of the chapter when I was speaking about my boss not realizing I was an introvert.

Not all successful salespeople are extreme extroverts that just have that knack for making people like them and selling a product/service. Anyone that says otherwise can quite frankly go kick rocks. (That's my rated G version side of me trying to calm the rated R version. How am I doing?)

Something that distinguishes a decent salesperson from a phenomenal salesperson is the ability to adapt and overcome. I like to coin the term as becoming a "chameleon" in the sales world. Chameleons have a wonderful survival mechanism that keeps them from becoming prey in the fight for their lives. Luckily, as human beings, we don't have as many predators to worry about when it comes to others being higher up on the food chain than us, but we do have other factors interpersonally to consider.

Being a great chameleon requires two things: know-how and practice. The know-how is provided in this chapter and is sprinkled throughout the book as well as other amazing resources. Applying that know-how is a completely different animal requiring experience and time. The battle is half done once you know who your "predators" are in regards to the personality types.

What I suggest is doing a little research project sometime. Look into the details of these four personality types and find a close friend or family member you know fits the role of each of the four personalities. Pick a random product and tell them you're going to try and sell it to them. Take note on how they react. What makes them agree with you and see value in the product you selected? What turns them off and pushes them away?

Ultimately, nothing can replace organic experience, but it never hurts to practice! You're constantly engaged in debate or sales techniques in day to day life when you're conversing among friends and family. You just don't realize it. It's happening when you're trying to convince your significant other on what you should do this weekend. The techniques are all there. Now you can actually be intentional with how you approach those conversations! (Side note: That advice didn't come from me if you get backlash from your spouse saying you're trying to psycho-analyze them. I plead ignorance and this book was never written.)

CHAPTER 8

PARADIGM SHIFT OF THE '3 V'S'

WITH THE BASIC principles in place for us to utilize, we can learn about the fine tuning of the process over the course of the next couple of chapters! We begin with the concept of 3 V's. The 3 V's of communication have been around for close to forty-five years now since they became popular and are still widely used by experts in the field today. I can recall my boss using it in our leadership development training not even four months ago! If it's been around for that long, it's probably worth looking into. We will dive into how the 3 V's impact each scenario of sales: In person and over the phone. It's also worth going through how that may shift as we transfer more into written forms of communication with social media taking a large foothold in today's society.

They grow up so Fast

Remember those nights when you were a kid where you'd have sleepovers and come up with the craziest ideas on how to keep yourselves entertained since you had an entire night with the guys? I remember one of those specific nights all too well. Sometimes, I really miss it not being the 'cool' thing as an adult. Who wouldn't love to still have sleepovers as an adult? (...Right?)

One particular afternoon, my brother and I were at a friend's house and drank entirely way too much Mountain Dew. Needless to say, we were a little ramped up and stir crazy. I equate it to how I feel now being in quarantine 30 days at home. Back to the point, though, we decided to find some old fireworks from the year prior and have some fun.

We grabbed some of the plastic toy action figures that were popular back then and decided we wanted them to ATTEMPT to go on a trip to outer space. So, we put our brain power together between the five of us and thought up how to strap the fireworks on, what type they'd be, where take off would happen, etc. It really was an elaborate game plan, if I do say so myself.

Once preparations were complete, we set off on our half mile hike to the fields nearby to get our launching pad prepared. That launching pad happened to be in the middle of a small grove of small shrubbery and trees on a concrete slab. It seemed like a great place at the time! We placed the 25 gallon bucket full of sparklers onto the concrete slab and strapped the heroic action figure with the bottle rocket in at the top of the mountain of sparklers. If we were going to do this, we wanted to make it flashy and do it right!

The countdown began from 10. It seemed like an eternity

until we hit the final count... *3... 2... 1...* TAKEOFF! That's when it struck me that maybe this wasn't such a good idea. But, it was a little too late for that.

We ran as fast as we could away from the launch pad. I'm not sure if you've ever lit $100 worth of sparklers at the same time before, but it's quite a sight once it gets going. It's the best ten second light show you've ever seen for that amount of money! Looking at it from twenty feet away, we were amazed as the sparklers finally lit up enough to light the entire bucket. That's when the twenty foot tall flash of fire came up... and lit one of the surrounding trees on fire.

The first thought that went through my head wasn't on how to save the tree that was now on fire or how much trouble I was going to get into with the local authorities. It was what my father was going to do when he found out.

Fast forward to when that happened... because, it did and it wasn't pretty. I remembered dad looking at me with that fit of rage and disappointment. I quite honestly don't even have the slightest clue what he actually said to me. Seriously. All I remember was the look in his eyes and the eruption of rage from his mouth. Who knew that would actually make a great story for the topic of communication years and years later. That night was a prime example as to how the 3 V's are relevant in any communication. Let's see how.

Albert Mehrabian's 3 V's

The 3 V's of communication are verbal, vocal and visual. Verbal relates to what we <u>actually say</u> and what comes out of our mouth when we speak. Vocal is how we <u>sound</u> when we say it. Visual is how we <u>look</u> when we say what we are saying. Let's look at the breakdown below to see how much impact each factor makes. If you haven't heard this theory or seen it before, it's pretty eye opening. Those that have, hopefully this is a good refresher or a different take on it.

<u>Verbal</u> = 7%
<u>Vocal</u> = 38%
<u>Visual</u> = 55%

If we refer back to the end of the story that I'm not proud of, what did you notice? Re-read it and look at my personal recollection of it. Does it coincide with the percentages above? A whopping 55% of our engagement with another person is interpreted based on how we LOOK when we say something and an additional 38% off of how we SOUND. That means what we actually say accounts for only 7% of the interpretation of the entire conversation.

Those are some pretty staggering numbers when you look at sales and your presentations. Obviously, it is extremely important to still choose the right wording (if you recall us spending time going through that in the psychology of sales). However, where most people miss the mark is relative to more of the visual and vocal side of things. Let's break those two down a bit more so we can know how to improve upon those two key areas.

Visual:

How you look when you say something is extremely important. Even though you may not realize it, you are constantly paying attention to small visual cues when you speak to someone. Ever had a time when you were speaking with someone and their eyes kept darting off on things that were going on around you? Did it bother you when they kept deviating from being engaged in the conversation with you? How about when you're speaking to someone, but they don't nod or smile and just sit there with a stoic look on their face? Ever had that happen before? One more for good measure. Have you ever had a time when someone spoke to you with their arms across their chest and laid back in their chair? It was probably your dad telling you that you were crazy and weren't going to get what you were asking for when you were a kid! (I do not speak from experience.)

All of these situations listed above happen ALL of the time and even happen in professional conversations and settings. They greatly impact the outcome of a conversation whether it's intentional or not. Being aware of how you LOOK when you speak to someone can have a huge impact on the outcome of that discussion, both positive and negative.

When listening, this becomes extremely important. Your eyes and your smile are two of the most powerful tools in your arsenal when it comes to being an active listener in a conversation. Having eyes locked in on the person in front of you and smiling while doing nods where necessary gives the speaker the capability to see that you're engaged and active in the conversation you are having. Your stance and how you present your physical body both play a huge role as well.

Practicing this with a friend/spouse/family member is a great way to improve in this area. As weird as it may sound, I've personally had family and co-workers videotape me from both the speaker's perspective as well as the listener perspective. You'd be amazed what you pick up on that you don't notice you do until someone points it out to you or you see it yourself on video footage! Everyone has visual fidgety actions they do when they are nervous, anxious, rushed, etc. Write down what you see so you can work on and improve them.

Vocal:

How you SOUND when you say something is almost as important as how you look when you say it. When my father found out what we had done in the example above, the very next thing that I noticed after the look on his face was the tone and sound of his voice. My fight or flight instinct told me to run and never, ever, look back! Unfortunately, I had no other homes sitting around that I could live in, so I took it as well as any young adult male would. I'm still alive to write this book, so it must not have been THAT bad.

There are a few primary components to consider when thinking about how you sound when you say something. Those 3 components are your volume, tone, and clarity. I'm sure the tone of my voice elevated and had some voice inflection when I had to respond to my dad in regards to his question of *what in the @$*_ I was thinking when I did that?!* I distinctly remember the volume of his voice elevating drastically, indicating that he wasn't very happy with me. The clarity of his words, "*You. Will. Not. Ever. Do. That. Again"* were very concise and clear. The pauses between each word added the dramatic effect for that clarity.

The same goes for sales when you're speaking to a prospect about solving a problem that they need fulfilled with your product/service. Do you have excitement in your voice without being over the top? Do you effectively make use of increasing volume during times of importance or you need to build excitement? Small details like this seem miniscule, but can add up to create an entirely different experience for the individual working with you.

Verbal:

Lastly, what you actually say plays a role as well. I won't dwell and spend a ton of time here, since we went over this thoroughly among some of the other chapters. The person in front of you is the largest factor to consider when thinking about WHAT words you want to say. Are they younger or older? White collar or blue collar? What type of personality are they among the four we listed earlier? There are numerous factors that play a role in how you will speak when talking to someone and what list of vocabulary to use.

We consider these factors, because we want to more easily connect with the individual in front of us as well as make it easy for them to understand the value in what we are offering for the need they have.

For example, what if you personally just stepped foot into a fitness center for the first time and the person trying to get you started on your journey has a doctorate in Exercise Physiology and Dietetics and just starts spewing off facts about high level ways to fine tune your programming? Sure, it might sound pretty cool, but if it's your very first time making a lifestyle change in health and wellness, do you think that you're going to connect to someone speaking way above your head and talking about things you haven't even thought of doing yet? You just want to be consistent and learn how to move those lever arms on the machines, for crying out loud!

This is where WHAT you say becomes important. It helps create the context for the conversation and allows a bridge to be built between you and the prospect to help build that rapport and find common ground.

Wrapping it up:

When you put all three aspects of communication together, it creates an entire art form of its own. Sales is a subtle art, and communication is a subtle art within sales that takes practice, and a lot of it. If you can master the 'gift of gab' as a former colleague of mine used to say, then your ability to create a positive experience for everyone you meet is elevated to another level.

How does this change over the phone and on non-visual outlets?

Albert Mehrabian's 3 V's research model was provided given an 'in-person' interaction. As the world changes... And one given is that the world will NEVER stop changing; we have to consider how that impacts where our focus must be in regards to communication among other areas. Luckily for us, phones were already around when Albert was doing his research and the numbers are there for phone conversation.

When talking over the phone, 84% of communication is vocal and 16% of it is verbal. If you recall the equation earlier, verbal communication only accounted for 7%. What's the biggest takeaway from this? What you <u>say</u> over <u>doubles</u> in importance, which is no surprise since the visual is completely taken out of the equation. However, the more staggering statistic to me is that 84% of the communication is still vocal. How you sound when you're on the phone is the most important factor to consider.

Think about a scenario where you had to be extremely

empathetic for someone and convey that in a genuine manner. It's dark, but imagine someone close to you just had their child pass away unexpectedly. That's an extremely tough situation to be in. If you were the family member that had to help comfort them, how would your interaction change to convey empathy and support if you had to do it over the phone?

This is where tone and voice inflection become so important and why individuals who haven't practiced and developed vocal skill sets have issues building rapport within a relationship, whether it's for personal or sales purposes. There's no secret formula to improve this other than practice and self-awareness.

Stepping into the future

No one can fully predict where the future will take us when it comes to communication and the 3 V's, but I can say two things:

1. Everything in this book and everything for normal sales will ALWAYS apply, because sales is about building relationships and being able to understand people and their needs. Foundationally, that will never change.

2. If you're genuine, practice your craft, and love what you do... the sky's the limit with your success. Read - learn - grow: Spend time honing in on opportunities and make sure you accentuate your strengths and use them to your advantage.

The world of social media has completely changed the dynamic of how salespeople can operate and function. At Life Time, my current employer, we have an entire staff for each region of the country fully dedicated to online sales and web traffic management. They do a heck of a job doing it.

The question is, what helps them be successful in what they do? Below are some key things to think about regarding online communication:

- Be concise and to the point. It's easy to word "vomit" and can cause a disconnect and boredom.

- Don't argue over online mediums. Not going to elaborate on this. Just don't.

- Use proper punctuation, spelling and grammar. Especially when it's a professional setting.

- Don't use caps lock or overuse emojis and other icons.

- Be aware of wording used and ensure the context matches what you want to convey.

- Lastly - written and online-based communication is meant to be an additive into your sales day. It is not a substitute for phone/in person conversation. Use it until you can verbally speak to someone or talk to them in person.

The point of any communication form is to build rapport, value and interest. I use online mediums to communicate with those that may not speak over phone or in person initially and leverage that to build enough rapport and trust to get them to come speak to me personally or over the phone.

Now that you have an understanding of what impacts conversation and what to look out for, it's time to go get some video taping in. Get your friends and family involved and have fun with it!

CHAPTER 9

IN-PERSON SALES VS. IN-HOME SALES

IN TODAY'S SOCIETY (especially at this moment, being under quarantine due to the Coronavirus) where the world's technology is exponentially growing, a large number of individuals that normally would not have launched themselves into the sales world are now wanting to create another source of income for themselves and their families. This has become a widespread phenomenon in a very short period of time. Did you know that 1 in 13 adults over the age of 18 had invested time in an MLM/from home business in 2019?

This is a double edged sword, in my experience and opinion. On the one side, how amazing is it that absolutely anyone with internet access has the ability to reach anyone, anywhere in the world, and sell them a product or service they can make commissions on? It's quite amazing, honestly.

On the other side of the blade, though, are the false hopes and lack of preparation. You have individuals that come in with the mentality that they are going to become super-rich in a matter of a few months. What they don't realize is that those who make money in these businesses are investing a LOT of time in not only their customers, but in developing their downlines and ensuring they have successful business models as well. It's a grind that a lot of people aren't usually willing to take. The presentations usually don't focus on that side of the business.

The point of this chapter is not to debate whether MLM's are good or bad for you. The point is to dive into how you can be successful in one that is the right fit for YOU. Since statistics are pretty skewed based on data collected, I'll leave you with one statistic. 50% of affiliates usually leave the organization within one year of joining.

Why do I point out this specific fact? Have you ever personally seen someone grow a mega-million dollar business in under a year before? If you have, let's have coffee and go through what their business plan was. I can guarantee it's not going to be a model that can be duplicated by many individuals.

Where I'm going with this is this... Success takes time in sales. It's about building relationships and building recognition. It's a snowball effect that requires consistency and grit. The reason so many people fail at MLM's is not necessarily due to the business model (though I do urge that you deep dive into the one you are looking into), but more so because the affiliate didn't grasp and comprehend the level of work and the art behind becoming great at it. That, or they didn't have a leader in their upline that had a well drawn-out process that could be duplicated.

Blending Multi-Level-Marketing Sales & Standard Sales

The question that's on your mind right now is: *How do I become successful at MLM sales? What do I have to do that's different from normal sales?*

That's a very good question - I'm glad you asked! I'll let you in on a little secret. It's not too different from in-person, normal everyday sales. The principles behind selling on the MLM stage and direct sales jobs are EXACTLY the same. It comes down to the exact two major principles discussed at the beginning of the book. <u>Are you able to build value in/emotion towards your product/service and make them see it's the BEST way to fulfill that need they have? Secondly, are you able to build rapport and trust to the point where they feel like a dick if they say no to you?</u>

That's it. Plain and simple. Just like 'normal' sales, if you can do those two things extremely well. You will see success if you manage your business properly. Simple enough, right? Not quite.

There's one major difference when it comes to MLM performance vs. single-level in person sales. Your team and downline comes into play with MLM's. For the sake of this book, we are going to focus on a high level since every company is different and has different structures. The core foundations of how MLM's work will be very similar, though. That's our focus here.

MLM *differences*

Multi-level-marketing is exactly what it sounds like. It's built to have tiers. You make money via two primary paths… Your personal sales being the first path. The second path is your 'downline' and their sales. Most companies will give you a percentage of commissions based on your downline's ability to sell and then pay you for your personal sales as well.

So how does this all become relevant for what we want to discuss within here? In order to be successful in MLM sales, you have a different skill-set that has to be developed. That skillset is your ability to coach, inspire and mentor other affiliates to do the exactly same thing you are doing. Much like I am doing right now! This adds another level into the mix. Not only do you have to be good at selling the product/service, you also have to be good at presenting to others to inspire them to jump on the opportunity. (Or find someone that is great at presenting and you just get them in front of that person.)

The principles behind getting prospects inspired aren't much different from how you'd get a potential prospect inspired to purchase your product itself! They have to have a need that needs to be fulfilled and you have to be able to fill that need with what you have to offer and convince them that YOUR offer is the best one. If they aren't bought into that, does your presentation allow them to see the value in the product itself to allow them to become customers of yours?

The key to MLM success becomes finding a couple of solid stand out players that are willing to grind and have the tenacity and personality to be great at selling themselves. You then help them find a few players that can be the support on their team, etc. If you focus on building a great team, the customers will organically come from individuals you speak with that may say no to becoming part of the team, but see value in the product. Never sacrifice one for the other when considering the experience they are getting during your presentations. Outside of that, it's business as usual.

Just like every single sports coach always says, "*You can't win without a solid foundation. That foundation has to be getting extremely good at the basics.*" Teach your team to do the same thing you're doing, and you will see success.

CHAPTER 10

BUILDING YOUR BOOK OF BUSINESS

BEING ABLE TO learn sales skill sets is all groovy and awesome until you realize you have no one around you to sell to. First off, you have to have a product/service that fulfills a need that people have. If that isn't crossed off the list, you're going to have a hard time selling anything. Make sure you practice healthy hygiene habits as well. I've never seen an amazing salesperson that didn't have great hygiene. No one wants to smell you.

Great! Now that we have that aside, how do we build a book of business now that we have the foundation for success once they are in front of us? I saved this chapter for later in the book for a specific reason: You probably wouldn't even be starting your journey in sales if you read this chapter earlier on in the book. Now that you've invested enough time into it, the chances of making you successful have increased substantially. See how I worked you? Boom. Sales.

Building a book of business is NOT a fast OR easy process.

It takes time, commitment, grit, thick skin, gift of gab, etc. You get the point. Let's go into the facts of building a book of business and then break down how to attack those.

- You need "street cred" that proves you know what you're talking about

- You need raving fans to promote you - Hard to do when you don't have a book of business already

- You need accessibility and coverage

- You need a network of people

So... we need to be an expert in the field, get raving fans, be accessible and have a network of people we can team up with to build an even larger network of people we can meet and reach out to. Can't be too bad, right?!

The first thing that becomes extremely important in sales is knowing your target audience and their needs as well as knowing your product. This is something that takes time and energy. Ever heard the saying, "Rome wasn't built in a day"? Of course you have. And it's a grossly overused statement for a reason. Rome really wasn't built in a day. It took the effort and teamwork of a LOT of people.

Just as in Rome, your book of business will not take off on day one. The process doesn't have to be complicated though! Knowing your product and how that product impacts/helps the needs of the consumer is paramount to begin that process. You wouldn't want a plumber trying to give advice/selling medical equipment that has a life saving impact, would you? You would definitely use them to give you ideas on how to fix that leak under your sink or tell you why mold is showing up in your walls, though. Same with you and your industry, you have to study and perfect your craft.

Once that is complete, you need to showcase your skills and knowledge through public mediums. Write to the local newspaper on concerns in your field, start a blog, launch a podcast, volunteer in local events and give to a cause to get your name out there. The more exposure you can get through providing good content to people in your field, the better. People want to know you know your stuff, but they also want to know that you care enough about them that you're willing to support them even if they haven't purchased a product.

Taking that one step further, once you start to build that 'street cred' as we call it, you can start to pursue other outlets as well. Getting a place online put together where prospects and consumers can know more about your product/service (ie. website, facebook business, instagram business, etc) is a great place to start. Utilizing public speaking on topics relative to your product/service is another amazing way. Expos, large city events, chambers of commerce... events and places like that are always looking for experts in the field to speak at events.

Participating through the outlets above will also help you get to know people in your field and other fields as well with like-minded goals. This is where your networking truly starts and takes off. This is why you often see MLM salespeople hyping up their friends in other small businesses online to help support them. If you can support one another, why wouldn't you? It's a win/win!

Taking it to the next level:

Once you start networking with others, making connections, and becoming an expert in the field... you can begin to get those first initial clients rolling in. This is where building your book of business truly shines and takes off.

Let's use an example. My first fitness sales job was at 24 Hour Fitness. When I first started, I had just moved to the city. I knew no one, and no one knew or cared who I was. So I started where I needed to. I built credibility. Little did I know that the credibility had been in the making over the last 10 years of my life committing myself to a healthy lifestyle. *Insert announcer voice here*

Weighing in at 270 pounds at 10% body fat - A man that came from the bowels of insecurity; hailing from a former body of 150 pounds soaking wet... A man that overcame the naysayers and doubters... A man that stood the test of time... I present to you: BRIAN LAUDICK.

I may have dramatized that a little bit to drive the point home, but you get the point. If you don't, here it is: I was a walking billboard for my product/service. Directly out of the gate, I had a degree in the field. I had spent 5 days a week participating in sports and working out since the age of 4. This wasn't an overnight preparation. It was my life preparing me for this role. Now I just had to use that to my advantage.

I did so with humility and genuine kindness. It started with that very first sale. To prevent boring you, I'll fast forward. My first prospect bought a membership, they got engaged with training, and they became a walking billboard for me. This is the turning point in the game where salespeople stay stagnant or leap over the chasm into longevity and success: Referrals from existing clients.

Give someone an amazing experience and they'll, on average, tell nine people about that experience, depending on the source you look at. What does that mean for you? It means more potential clients and more money to put on your family's table. And that process exponentially increases, if you are consistent in your processes and your care factor. By the way,

I'd get your highlighter out or tablet if you don't already have it handy, because this is where your business truly takes off.

Let's go back to 24 Hour Fitness, when I was a Sales Manager for them and had the most amazing team in place with me. I started off in the position with zero referrals. Fresh from the ground up.

I took every opportunity in as if it were my baby. It was a new chance to impress someone and give them a WOW moment in their day that they couldn't help but talk about. I didn't stop there with just their experience that day. It continued on with their support after the sale, the conversations in passing, the holiday cards, etc. I took personal responsibility to ensure the person in front of me not only got closed, but they got the treatment and plan of attack they deserved.

Fast forward to nine months later, when I left the role for a promotion to become a General Manager for the company. Remember that amazing sales team I was a part of at the time? It was one of the hardest days for me to work the last day with them. We were family.

One of the great things I left behind for them as I took the next step in my journey was my lead database. You will recall that I started with zero referrals in my pipeline. When I left, there were over seven-hundred people I had names and contact information for that had been REFERRED to me by satisfied consumers. Over seven-hundred that I had not even been able to reach out to yet due to having such a high volume. That's lead generation that you can't get anywhere else for such a low cost (ie. free since you don't have to pay for any marketing whatsoever.)

Coming around full circle:

This is where the revelation of sales is born. Every single chapter leading up to this point has discussed the process of the sale and how to build relationships. Why is that? Because, the most important part of any salesperson's world is the clientele. Without prospects, we don't have a job.

We can be the smartest marketing gurus on the planet and have all the fancy bells and whistles at our disposal to get people in front of us, but a thousand things can go wrong after that to stall your progress and give your client a bad taste in their mouth. That bad experience for one client can lead to them telling fifteen to twenty other people about that experience, which is something you CANNOT afford to have happen. This is why the process, and the art of sales is so important. Without a solid process and foundational 'why' behind what you do, the experience suffers. Referrals from existing clients are the number one way to build the 'snowball effect' in your book of business that I keep talking about. Ask anyone that's been in the same sales position for longer than five years. Ask them where they get most of their leads. I guarantee it's not from Facebook ADs (albeit, that is a great way to jump start getting leads in front of you at the start.)

It's from doing two things so phenomenally well that the prospect feels like a dick if they say no to you. (Holy cow - the title of this book coming to full fruition. IT'S NUTS, I TELL YOU!)

1. No matter the service or product, make someone emotionally charged about what you're selling. Humans are emotional creatures. The power of emotion is very persuasive and is critical in the buying process. They

have to see the value on how it will impact their lives and be able to envision that.

2. Build so much rapport and common ground with the potential buyers, entrenched in a genuine connection, that is strong enough to make them feel like a dick if they have to say no to you.

Your book of business is out there for the taking. Are you ready to get this party started? (No alcohol in this party, if you're under 21 and reading this. Sorry!)

CHAPTER 11

COFFEE'S FOR CLOSERS:
FINAL NOTES

ENVISION YOUR FUTURE self with me here for a moment. You've lived a full and healthy life. Let's say you're on a train… to quote *Inception*. You're on a train that will take you far away at the end of your life. You know where you HOPE this train will take you, but you can't know for sure. When you're on that train at the end of your life, how do you want to look back at it?

This isn't some fluffy feel good question to get you in the mood. I'm serious. What do you want to look back at and be remembered by? Your looks? Fame? Being an amazing parent? A faithful spouse? Whatever it is that you want to be remembered as, that version of you started yesterday. It's continuing here at this moment as you read this book. That version of you is going to have the opportunity to shine tomorrow when you wake up as well.

Tomorrow is never guaranteed, though. So I ask you now: what are you doing to help yourself and others around you? What are you going to accomplish TODAY that allows you to fulfill your personal needs in life? No one can sell you that, unfortunately. It's something that cannot be bought. It's something that has to be earned and can only be done by you.

Whatever it is that you want to do in life and be remembered by, I only ask one thing of you as you're reading this… Whether you're religious or not, the thing I'm about to ask of you comes from a line in one of my favorite books. 'Chase the Lion'. It's a great book to buy and read for life motivations, by the way.

So here it is… I ask that you quit living life as if the purpose of life is to safely arrive at death. ***Go after a*** <u>dream</u> ***that is destined to FAIL without divine intervention.*** Why? Because, if it isn't destined to fail without intervention, it's not a large enough dream. The chances of you even being born are 1/400 trillion. The fact that you're even here reading this book is a gift. Why would you waste any time not exploring everything life has to offer and fully taking advantage of it not only for yourself, but also in helping others?

Why the soapbox?

I say all of this for one reason. Too many people are mediocre at things they do, and that includes those in sales. And a lot of them live normal lives and die, but if you are reading this book then you're not just satisfied with waking up and breathing. You need more. You can have more and unlock more in life. Every single tactic, cue, technique and pointer in this book can help you become an amazing salesperson, if you apply the knowledge.

If you look at it from an "outside of sales" lens, it can help you reshape the rest of your life as well. A majority of people that attempt sales will fail. It's not an easy field to be a part of.

That's why I love it so much. It's a challenge just like life is a challenge. It's a challenge that uses *people* as the catalyst. That's what sales is all about. Building relationships and nurturing those relationships. Life is about the very same thing, ironically enough.

The question becomes, will you develop the skill sets to be great at building genuine relationships? If so, you'll begin to notice a lot of positive changes in your life. Organically, your sales business will flourish as a healthy side effect.

Closing it all out:

We've covered a lot of ground in this book that you can now take and introduce into your own personal style of selling. If I could recommend one last thing in closing it would be this: make it your own. At the end of it all, we are actors on a stage and have a role to play in the grand scheme of life.

Your story is meant to be different from mine or anyone else's. Heck, I hope I get an email or note from you someday, letting me know how business is going and what changed in your life and how you molded this knowledge into your own personal brand. Be you, because no one else is as good at it as you are.

And as you're sitting there years down the road, on that train that you hope leads to where you want it to at the end of life…Sipping the coffee that you rightfully deserve… I hope you say, "*You know what, Brian? I wasn't a dick!*" If so, then my job here is done and writing all of this was worth every second it took. Because it meant changing your life in such a way that it inspired you to change other lives in the same manner.

I still look back on my journey and how it's progressed as the days go by. Sometimes, I still feel like I'm that insecure

150lb skinny boy that was too afraid to step outside of his comfort zone to achieve anything worthy of praise. Yet, here we are in this moment.

Life is a journey of amazing ups and downs. Each experience is there to prepare you for the next chapter of your journey. I never thought I'd be writing a book on sales and launching a platform that would help mentor others to build relationships and positively influence their lives too. But, every scenario I was put in has built me up for this. Just like it will for you. Let's be real, if this introvert can write a book and be successful in sales, anyone can.

Now it's your turn to write your story. The amazing thing is it has already begun and the culmination of your experiences have led you here on purpose. You've already been writing your own story and forging your own path. Hopefully, this allows you to have that next defining moment in your life where you take the fork in the road that's less traveled. Thanks for reading and joining on the journey of sales. It's now time to write the next chapter of *your* journey.

Made in the USA
Coppell, TX
04 August 2021

59961700R00056